The Life and World of

TUTANKHAMEN

Brian Williams

www.heinemann.co.uk/library
Visit our website to find out more information about Heinemann Library books.

To order:
☎ Phone 44 (0) 1865 888066
📄 Send a fax to 44 (0) 1865 314091
💻 Visit the Heinemann Library Bookshop at www.heinemann.co.uk/library to browse our catalogue and order online.

First published in Great Britain by Heinemann Library,
Halley Court, Jordan Hill, Oxford OX2 8EJ
a division of Reed Educational and Professional Publishing Ltd.
Heinemann is a registered trademark of Reed Educational & Professional Publishing Ltd.

OXFORD MELBOURNE AUCKLAND
JOHANNESBURG BLANTYRE GABORONE
IBADAN PORTSMOUTH (NH) USA CHICAGO

© Reed Educational and Professional Publishing Ltd 2002
The moral right of the proprietor has been asserted.

Designed by Celia Floyd
Illustrated by Jeff Edwards and Joanna Brooker
Originated by ambassador Litho Ltd
Printed by Wing King Tong in Hong Kong.

ISBN 0 431 14761 2
06 05 04 03 02
10 9 8 7 6 5 4 3 2 1

British Library Cataloguing in Publication Data

Williams, Brian, 1943–
    The life and world of Tutankhamen
    1. Tutankhamen, Pharaoh of Egypt   2. Pharaohs – Biography – Juvenile literature
    3. Egypt – History – Eighteenth dynasty, ca.1570–1320 B.C. – Juvenile literature
    I. Title   II. Tutankhamen
    932'.014'092

Acknowledgements

The Publishers would like to thank the following for permission to reproduce photographs: Ancient Art and Architecture: p17; The Art Archive: pp5, 6, 9, 10, 11, 12, 14, 15, 16, 20, 22, 26, 27; Corbis: pp7, 8, 18, 21; The Griffiths Institute: pp23, 24, 28; Hilary Fletcher: p13; Hulton Archive: p29; Werner Foreman Archive: pp19, 25. Cover photograph reproduced with permission of

Cover photograph reproduced with permission of Corbis.

Our thanks to Rebecca Vickers for her comments during the preparation of this book.

Every effort has been made to contact copyright holders of any material reproduced in this book. Any omissions will be rectified in subsequent printings if notice is given to the Publisher.

Contents

Any words appearing in the text in bold, **like this**, are explained in the glossary.

Gift of the Nile

This is the story of a **pharaoh**, or king, of Egypt, who lived more than 3000 years ago. Egyptian kings before Tutankhamen had conquered an empire, and left the biggest **monuments** ever built – the pyramids.

Tutankhamen was not one of these great kings. We know very little about his life, which ended before he was 20. And yet he is the most famous of all Egyptian kings, because in 1922 his **tomb** was discovered by the **archaeologist** Howard Carter. The tomb was full of the most amazing objects, which help us picture Tutankhamen's life and times. What Carter first saw by flickering candlelight still astonishes museum visitors. Tutankhamen's tomb was a time capsule, taking us back 3000 years.

▶ Egypt's rich civilization was made possible by the River Nile. Cities and farms were close to the river. Northern Egypt was called Lower Egypt; the southern part was Upper Egypt.

The land of Egypt

Tutankhamen's land was hot and dry, as Egypt still is today. A strip of desert was made green by the waters of the River Nile, flowing north from the heart of Africa. Every year the flooding Nile spread dark fertile soil along its banks, enriching the fields for farmers to grow food.

How do we know?

When Tutankhamen was alive, the pyramids were already over 1000 years old, but writings on temple walls listed kings dating far back before the pyramids. These tell us that about 5000 years ago, King Menes ruled Upper Egypt, and he conquered Lower Egypt. Tutankhamen became king about 2000 years later.

What we know about Tutankhamen comes from the study of the treasures found in his tomb, and from other discoveries made by archaeologists. Much is still unclear – who his parents were, for example. Even the dates of Tutankhamen's birth and death are not known for certain.

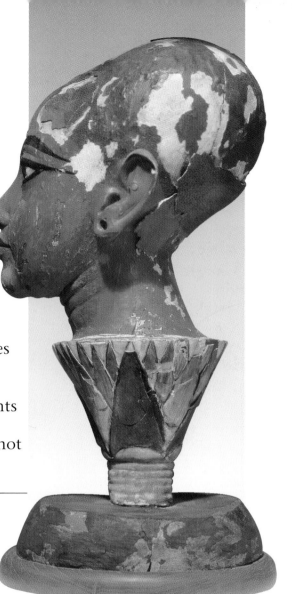

▶ A painted wooden head of Tutankhamen, who became king of Egypt when he was about 9 years old. He died about nine years later. The objects buried with him are clues to his life-story.

Key dates

3100 BC	King Menes rules all Egypt
2686–2181 BC	Great Pyramids built
1333–1323 BC	Tutankhamen rules Egypt
332 BC	Egypt conquered by Alexander the Great of Greece
69–30 BC	Life of Cleopatra, most famous queen of Egypt

Watch the dates

BC after a year date means before the birth of Jesus Christ. Historians are not sure about the dates of Tutankhamen's **reign**. You may see different dates in different books.

The Sun King's palace

Tutankhamen was born about 1342 BC in a new city of temples and palaces. The **pharaoh** Amenhotep IV had moved his entire court 500 kilometres (311 miles) north from the old capital, Thebes, to the building site for his new capital beside the River Nile.

Turning Egypt upside down

This builder-king had shocked his people by starting a new religion. He believed in a new Sun god, called the **Aten**. He had changed his name to Akhenaten, meaning 'one useful to Aten'.

Akhenaten had turned Egypt upside down. Egyptians had always worshipped **Amen** and many other gods. Now the king abandoned them and worshipped only one god. Instead of going to war like his soldier-father Amenhotep III, he built the beautiful new city he called Akhetaten, 'the horizon of Aten'. Today, its ruins can be seen at a small town called Tell El-Amarna.

▶ **Akhenaten and Queen Nefertiti are shown worshipping the Sun god, or Aten. Nefertiti shared her husband's new religion. She was the king's chief wife.**

Pharaoh Akhenaten

Akhenaten ruled Egypt from 1352 to 1336 BC. Sculptures show him with a long, sensitive face and swollen stomach – it is possible he suffered from a **genetic disease**. Akhenaten's favourite wife was Queen Nefertiti. She helped plan their garden-city. The couple had six daughters, who may have been Tutankhamen's half-sisters.

Who were Tutankhamen's parents?

This unusual ruler Akhenaten was probably Tutankhamen's father, though some historians think Tutankhamen may have been Akhenaten's younger brother. The Egyptian royal family was complicated because kings often married their sisters and even their daughters. The baby prince was named Tutankhaten, meaning 'living image of the Aten'. He changed it to Tutankhamen when he became king and restored Egypt's old gods, so that is what he is called in this book.

Akhenaten had two main wives, Nefertiti and Tutankhamen's mother Kiya. Kiya may have been a foreign princess. Even so, she was not as important as Nefertiti. She is not mentioned after the eleventh year of Akhenaten's reign, Maybe she died, perhaps when she gave birth to her son. Without modern medicines, childbirth could be a dangerous time for women, who prayed to the hippo-headed goddess Taweret to protect them.

▶ This stone carving shows Akhenaten and Nefertiti holding hands. Informal art like this was a feature of his reign.

The little prince

Pictures found in royal **tombs** show us family life in Egypt. The king's Great Palace was kept for official ceremonies. His family probably lived mostly in the North Palace. This must have been fun for little Tutankhamen, since **archaeologists** think it had its own zoo, with birds, antelopes and lions. There were family pets too – dogs, cats, monkeys and birds were favourite pets in Egypt.

The royal family at home

The palace walls were decorated with soft colours and painted scenes of wildlife and plants. Blank walls were given painted windows, to match the walls with real windows – the Egyptians liked balance.

Every day, as the people's **high priest**, the king had religious duties to perform. He also supervised the builders and artists working on new temples and tombs. While most Egyptians worked hard, the royal family lived in leisurely comfort. Servants washed the hands and feet of visitors, brought food and drink, and gently waved fans to create a cooling breeze. Tutankhamen's companions were probably the children of court officials and nobles.

▶ A statue of Tutankhamen as a child. Boys often had their heads shaved, except for a lock on one side. Tutankhamen wears the headdress of a prince.

Pleasures and sorrows

It must have been fun to be a **pharaoh's** son. Like other princes before him, Tutankhamen paddled boats on the palace lake and caught fish among the water lilies. Sitting in the shade of palm trees, he would have enjoyed his nurse's stories. One popular tale told how a toy crocodile turned into a real one when a naughty child threw it into the water! But for all Egyptians, daily life brought sorrows too. One of Tutankhamen's sisters, Merykaten, died giving birth to a baby. A tomb picture shows Akhenaten and Nefertiti looking sad, while a nurse holds the baby.

◀ Bes was a popular household god. A bearded dwarf, he protected children, killed poisonous snakes and helped the goddess Taweret when babies were being born.

Toys and games

From finds made by archaeologists, we know Egyptian children played with balls (some had seeds inside, so they rattled). They also had pull-along toys, such as toy mice with twitching tails and lions with snapping jaws. Pictures show games of leapfrog and tug-of-war. Four playing-boards, for a game called senet, were found in Tutankhamen's tomb. In another board game called snake, players moved counters to get to the snake's head in the middle.

9

Learning to rule

Tutankhamen would have been taught to read and write by **scribes**. He had to learn the many picture-signs or **hieroglyphs**, as well as a new 'everyday' writing being encouraged by the king. He was taught history, memorizing the names of the kings who had ruled before him. He stood beside his father to worship the **Aten**.

Lessons

Tutankhamen probably learned family history from Ay, an important government official who was possibly a relative of both the king and Queen Nefertiti. Lessons may have been held in the king's library, full of clay **tablets** and **papyrus scrolls**. There were maps of the empire to look at. Tutankhamen would certainly have learned about the calendar. His year had 365 days, just like ours.

▶ Egyptian scribes wrote on a kind of paper made from papyrus reeds, which grew along the banks of the River Nile. They also wrote on soft clay tablets, using a pointed stick.

In Egypt only boys went to school. Clever boys became priests or scribes, but most poor children started working as soon as they were big enough. Tutankhamen might well have crossed the Nile by boat to see the farmers growing food in the fields on the far bank. He would have toured the city's grainstores and workshops, and seen the crowded housing for the city workers.

Home life

Small children usually wore no clothes at all, but as Tutankhamen grew older his usual clothing would have been a short **kilt** made of **linen**, with **reed** or leather sandals on his feet. Women of the palace wore long dresses, dyed their hair, and wore make-up and jewellery.

The royal family ate their main meal in the cool of the evening. As they dined, musicians played on harps, flutes, drums, cymbals and rattles. At feasts, dancers twirled and acrobats tumbled to entertain the king and his guests. On hot nights, people slept on mats on the roof.

The Rosetta stone

Egyptian hieroglyphics remained a puzzle until 1799, when a French army officer unearthed a fragment of stone near Rosetta, east of Alexandria. The stone dates from about 180 BC, and on it is writing in hieroglyphics, everyday Egyptian writing, and Greek. By comparing the three scripts, a scholar named Jean François Champollion managed to read hieroglyphs for the first time.

▶ The Rosetta Stone records the good deeds of Ptolemy V.

The king is dead

Egypt was a land of **monuments**, such as the Great Pyramids and the colossal statues of Amenhotep III – the great king who may have been Tutankhamen's grandfather.

Who ruled next?

By the time Tutankhamen was 7, King Akhenaten may already have been ill. It seems he shared power with Smenkhkare, a mystery-prince who may have been the king's brother, or a son by another wife (and so Tutankhamen's half-brother). Some people even think Smenkhkare was Queen Nefertiti, under another name, but this does not seem very likely.

Akhenaten died about 1336 BC. He was not buried in the Valley of the Kings, the royal burial ground in the desert, but in a secret **tomb**. Smenkhkare also died within two or three years. In 1907 **archaeologists** found a tomb in the Valley of the Kings, which may be his. Tests on bones from a skeleton found in this tomb show that whoever was buried there could have been a brother of Tutankhamen.

▶ Akhenaten was a thinker and art-lover, not a soldier like his father Amenhotep.

▲ The Valley of the Kings lies in the desert on the west side of the River Nile. It is not far from the city of Luxor (ancient Thebes).

Tutankhamen is king

Tutankhamen was now king. He was 9 years old. Beside him stood the two most powerful men in Egypt, Ay the **counsellor** and Horemheb, commander of the army. Waiting in the shadows were the powerful priests of **Amen**. Now they saw their chance to bring back the old gods.

Preparing for death

Egyptians made careful preparations for death and the world they believed that people went to after death. To preserve bodies for this next world, they made **mummies**. The mummy was placed in a tomb, with things for the dead person to use in the next world. Some kings were buried in pyramids. Later, kings were buried in rock tombs in the Valley of the Kings. Most tombs were stripped bare by robbers, except for Tutankhamen's. Robbers broke into his tomb, but were chased away before they could take much. That is what makes it so precious.

The new king reigns

Although he was only 9, the new king was married at once. The Egyptians believed it was important for religious reasons for their king to be married to a person of equal rank. The wife chosen for Tutankhamen was Ankhesenpaten. She was the third of Akhenaten's six daughters, and so possibly Tutankhamen's half-sister. As was the custom, she had already been married to her father.

The old ways return

Although Tutankhamen **reigned**, he was too young to rule. He did what his advisers told him. He still worshipped the **Aten** in his father's city, but in the second year of his reign, he gave up his old name of Tutankhaten. His wife also replaced the *aten* part of her name with *amen*, as a further sign that the great god **Amen** was back in his rightful place.

Tutankhamen was not crowned king at once. His coronation by the high priests of Amen took place about three years later. He was crowned at the temple of Karnak, the main centre for worship of Amen. After this, he lived in palaces at nearby Thebes, once again Egypt's capital, and at Memphis. The priests probably showed him plans to make the **temples** of the old gods more magnificent than ever.

▶ Cartouches were oval frames around the names of kings, queens and gods. This shows Tutankhamen's cartouche. It is on the side of a **canopic** box.

A boy and his treasures

Too small for the royal throne, the boy-king probably still sat on a child's chair. Several chairs were buried with him. Artists brought him wonderful treasures, such as intricate jewellery set with gold, blue and red gemstones from the desert. Perhaps, though, he treasured family memories most. In his **tomb** were later placed an artist's palette belonging to his sister Merykaten, and a box-lid with a picture of another sister.

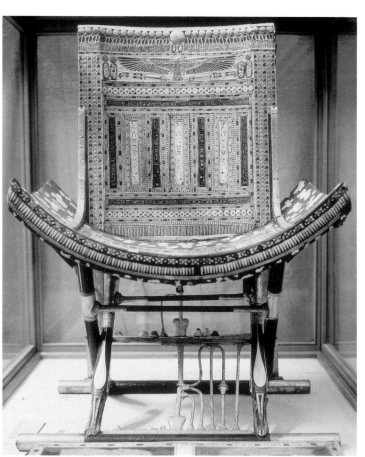

► This chair is so richly decorated with ebony, ivory and gold that it is called a throne. It is really a folding stool. On it are the names Tutankhaten and Tutankhamen.

Royal marriages

Marrying a daughter or a sister is not allowed by law now, but the Egyptians thought it made the king more like a god. Had Tutankhamen lived longer, he would probably have married other wives – a foreign princess, perhaps, or a **commoner**. Queen Tiy, wife of Amenhotep III, had been an important soldier's daughter.

Lord of all

Tutankhamen probably wanted to see for himself the land of which he was lord and master. The best way to travel was by boat along the Nile. The king would have relaxed beneath a canopy, shaded from the hot sun and fanned by servants. He would have been escorted by other boats carrying servants, guards, musicians, tents, food and drink. Belongings were packed in sacks, baskets and chests fastened with wooden locks or rope bindings. Horses and **chariots** followed along the shore, raising clouds of dust.

Life on the Nile

There was much to see – people fishing, farmers using **shadufs** to tip river water into ditches to water crops, boats laden with grain and vegetables, barges weighed down by blocks of building stone. In the shallows, men washed clothes, keeping a watchful eye open for crocodiles.

▶ Hunters in this tomb painting throw weighted sticks to catch wild ducks. Villagers kept tame ducks and geese for eggs. There were no chickens in Egypt.

Egyptian boats

Thirty-five miniature boats were found in Tutankhamen's tomb. Wood was scarce. Small boats were made from bundles of **papyrus reeds** lashed together with ropes. The king's river-boat was as big as the ships that traded across the Mediterranean and the Red Sea.

At night the royal party probably camped beside the river. Fish and wild duck made a tasty barbecue. The king might have tried his skill at duck-hunting, paddling a small boat through the reedbeds.

A *hunting trip*

A fan was found in Tutankhamen's **tomb**. On the fan handle, the king is pictured hunting ostriches. Writing on the handle tells us that the feathers for the fan were collected during a royal hunt. Hunting was a favourite sport in Egypt. It is likely that Tutankhamen would have gone hunting in the desert with his soldier-friends. As a boy, he would have been taught to drive a chariot and shoot a bow – a bow was found in his tomb. As king, he could pick the fastest horses, and his favourite hounds would have raced beside his chariot.

After the hunt, the royal party probably feasted on roast ostrich. Stretched on a camp bed in his tent, with musicians lulling him to sleep, the young king doubtless felt content to be lord of all.

▶ **Tutankhamen hunting ostriches is pictured in gold on the fan handle from his tomb. The ostrich feathers on the fan had been eaten away by insects.**

The might of Egypt

As **pharaoh**, Tutankhamen was commander-in-chief of Egypt's army. Kings sometimes led armies into battle, riding in war **chariots**. Pictures of these warlike kings with defeated prisoners reminded everyone of past glories. The young Tutankhamen would have been told of enemies, such as the **Hittites**. General Horemheb was keen to use the army to show the world that Egypt was still to be feared.

The king's army

The Egyptian army had many foot-soldiers. Soldiers were armed with **bronze** daggers and short swords, axes and clubs. They carried shields made of tough, dried ox-skin. Spearmen threw long spears tipped with copper or bronze points, and archers fired double-curved bows. The Egyptians had learned how to use these bows from their old enemies, the Hyksos, and bowmen could shoot arrows up to 400 metres. They rode into battle on horse-drawn chariots, fired into the enemy ranks, then raced away.

Horemheb led an army north into Lebanon and Palestine to fight the Hittites. He also fought against the **Nubians** in the south. Egypt was once again victorious. In **tomb**-pictures, Tutankhamen got the glory for these victories, but he probably never left Egypt himself.

▶ **This wooden figure shows Tutankhamen with a harpoon, as if about to spear a Nile hippopotamus. It was made for a religious ceremony.**

Tribute from abroad

One of Tutankhamen's officials was Huy, his governor in Nubia. In Huy's tomb there is a huge painting of him presenting visiting princes of Nubia to the boy-king. The Nubians brought rich gifts as **tribute**, including wild animals for the royal zoo. Perhaps Tutankhamen dreamed that one day he would drive in a chariot at the head of his army and see these distant lands for himself.

▲ The giraffe on this tomb painting is a tribute to the pharaoh. The foreigners offering it may be Nubians from the south.

Copper against iron

Although such an advanced people, the Egyptians were slow to use iron. The Hittites were the first to make iron swords and spears. Egyptian soldiers still used copper or **bronze** weapons, which easily snapped. A rare iron dagger was found in Tutankhamen's tomb.

Temple-builder

Every morning the young **pharaoh** would have gone to the **temple** to start the day.

Tutankhamen was restoring the old order. The priests once again wore leopard-skin cloaks (hidden away during Akhenaten's reign). Two cloaks, one of real leopard skin, one made of cloth, were found in Tutankhamen's tomb.

Return of the old gods

Ay, Tutankhamen's **counsellor**, encouraged this return to the old gods **Amen**, Re and Ptah. All three gods are shown on a trumpet found in Tutanhkamen's **tomb**. Ptah was the chief god of the old city of Memphis, and a wooden statue of this god was buried with Tutankhamun.

In official writings, the great Amenhotep III was now called Tutankhamen's 'father'. The new city of Akhetaten was abandoned. It was as if Akhenaten had never existed.

▲ This **papyrus scroll** shows what people believed happened after death. First, the jackal-headed god Anubis weighed the soul of a dead person against the ostrich feather of Ma'at, goddess of truth. The god Osiris then decided the fate of the soul.

▼ An adze for shaping wood, and other wooden and bronze tools used in temple-building around the time of Tutankhamen.

Building temples and tombs

New temples were built and old ones repaired. Many of the workers were prisoners of war. Massive blocks of stone were shipped along the Nile by barge, and then dragged overland on sledges. This is how the pyramids had been built over 1000 years earlier.

Treasurer Maya was the official in charge of the 'Place of Eternity', the Valley of the Kings. In this dry valley were the rock tombs of the pharaohs. Tutankhamen would one day join them, but work on his royal tomb had not yet begun. He might have been shown a small tomb being prepared for Ay – the counsellor was an old man.

Egyptian tools

Metal tools were so valuable that workers had to return them to the site store at the end of the day. The tools were weighed on balance scales morning and evening, to make sure that crafty workers were not chipping off bits of metal to melt down and sell.

The Nile floods

To Egyptians, the Nile was simply 'the river'. Every year in July the waters of the Nile began to rise, swollen by heavy rains in the tropical heart of Africa. The people rejoiced. This flood was welcomed, not feared. Without it, there would be no crops, no food, no life in Egypt.

The king led the ceremony of thanksgiving. He praised the gods for bringing new life to the parched land and asked for a rich harvest. Still wet, the black soil was turned by wooden ploughs pulled by oxen. This dark soil gave Egypt its name – Kemet, 'the black land'.

Farming in Egypt

Farmers either owned or rented small farms which belonged to large estates, held by the king. Government officials visited every farm twice a year, first to count fields and animals, and later to collect part of the harvest. This part went to feed the rest of Egypt's workers.

As a small boy, Tutankhamen had no doubt watched farmers working in the fields. The sowers sprinkled seed from baskets, and then sheep and goats were driven across the fields, to tread in the seed with their hooves.

▶ The top picture shows Egyptian farmers making haystacks at harvest time. The grain stalks were cut with sickles, edged with sharp flints. Below, grains are separated from stalks by pulling them through combs.

The most important crops were wheat, used to make flour for bread-making, and barley, for brewing beer. Flax was grown, to make **linen**. Dates were harvested in August, and were a favourite dessert. They were dried in the sun to preserve them. Dates and grapes were made into wine. Honey collected from beehives was used to sweeten foods.

Thanking the river god

When the harvest was gathered, Tutankhamen and his queen gave thanks to the river-god, Hapi. The **pharaoh** offered gifts of food, ornaments and jewels to the god's statue.

▲ There was meat for Tutankhamen to eat in the oval wooden boxes found in his tomb.

Food in Egypt

In the palace, people dined on beef, lamb and wild antelope. Poor people did not often eat meat. They ate mainly bread and vegetables, with fish or birds as a treat. Egyptians grew beans, lentils, lettuces, onions, leeks, melons, cucumbers and pomegranates. They loved figs – but so did wild baboons, which farmers chased away! In Tutankhamen's **tomb** there were 116 baskets of food and 30 jars of wine.

A brief reign ends

Pictures of Tutankhamen and his queen show a happy couple, but this happiness was short-lived. Tutankhamen prayed for a son, to succeed him. Twice the queen was pregnant, but each time the babies were born dead. Sorrowfully, the king and queen grieved as the tiny bodies were **mummified**. The babies were later buried with their father.

About 1323 BC, Tutankhamen died. The exact date is not known, and how he died is a mystery. Examination of his mummy found no proof that he was sickly. He was slim, about 1.65 metres tall, and his bones and teeth show that he was 17 or 18 years old. X-rays did reveal a tiny piece of bone chipped from his skull. He may have fallen from his **chariot**. Just possibly, he was murdered.

Becoming a mummy

After his death, the young king was handed over to the **embalmers**, for his body to be mummified. This took 70 days, and not until then could the funeral take place. The embalmers removed the vital organs (brain, stomach, liver and intestines). Usually these organs were put into **canopic** jars, but Tutankhamen's were buried in four miniature **coffins**. The heart remained in the body.

▶ **The mummy of Tutankhamen. Only one royal mummy had been found in its tomb before. The body inside the decayed linen wrappings was poorly preserved.**

The body was treated with salts, and packed with linen, sawdust or dry **lichen**. Painted stone eyes were placed in the eye-sockets. The body was rubbed with lotions and oils. Then it was wrapped in cloth. The dead king's fingers and toes were individually bandaged and a gold mask was made to cover his face.

Furniture, treasures, food and other items were collected to go into the dead king's **tomb**. All was then ready for the funeral.

▲ Tutankhamen's **shrine** was decorated with scenes. Some of these show him and his queen together. In this scene, the king pours water into the queen's cupped hand.

Furniture

Furniture put into Tutankhamen's tomb included lamps, jars, chests, beds and chairs. Royal furniture was much grander than the simple wooden tables and stools in poor people's homes. The king's small chair was made of ebony wood, imported from Africa. There were eight beds in the tomb – one a folding camp-bed – and four headrests, one made of **ivory**. Egyptians did not use pillows.

Buried and forgotten

Tutankhamen's **mummy** was taken across the Nile by boat to the Valley of the Kings. It was buried in a small **tomb**, maybe intended for Ay, as no royal tomb was ready. On the tomb walls are paintings showing the young king's welcome by the gods. One picture shows Ay, wearing a priest's leopard-skin cloak, performing a ceremony called the 'Opening of the Mouth' to prepare the dead king for the afterlife.

A vast crowd probably watched the funeral procession, as the king's mummy was carried into the tomb, but only eight people attended the funeral banquet. The flower-collar or wreath worn by one of them was to be a vital clue to rediscovering Tutankhamen's tomb.

▲ Ay (on the right) performs the Opening of the Mouth ceremony on Tutankhamen in this painting from the burial chamber.

What happened next

After Tutankhamen's death, his queen needed to remarry. She wrote to the **Hittite** king seeking a husband, and a Hittite prince came to Egypt, where he was murdered at once – probably on the orders of General Horemheb. Poor Queen Ankhesenpaten had to marry the ageing Ay. Ay became the new king.

Tutankhamen's tomb was closed, but robbers broke in at least twice and stole some jewellery and other items. One thief left his footprint on a white box, still visible 3000 years later. **Treasurer** Maya acted swiftly to close the tomb up again. Perhaps he guarded it for the rest of his life.

Tutankhamen vanishes from history

Ay ruled Egypt for only four years. When the old man died, he was buried in a new tomb, probably meant for Tutankhamen. Horemheb made himself **pharaoh** and tried to destroy all traces of the past. Ay's tomb was smashed. Tutankhamen's name was scratched off **monuments**. The **temple** of the **Aten** was pulled down. The boy-king's tomb was hidden by rubble, and soon both the tomb and Tutankhamen himself were forgotten.

▲ Tutankhamen was buried in three **coffins**, one inside the other. The two outer ones were made of wood, richly decorated with gold. The innermost coffin weighed 110 kg and was made of solid gold. This painting on the wall of Tutankamen's tomb shows the king being welcomed by a goddess.

The mummy hunters

Foreigners began visiting the Valley of the Kings 2000 years ago when Roman tourists inspected empty tombs. Mummies were sold as curiosities, but the Egyptians hid many of the royal mummies. When Howard Carter opened Tutankhamen's tomb, 33 royal tombs were known in the Valley of the Kings, but all had been robbed long ago. More tombs have since been found.

Wonders revealed

In 1907 an American named Theodore Davis was **excavating** in the Valley of the Kings. His team found a cup with Tutankhamen's name on it, some scraps of gold foil with pictures of the **pharaoh**, and pottery jars left over from a funeral. In one jar were faded floral collars. Could these be clues to finding a lost **tomb**?

Howard Carter took up the search. He was a British **archaeologist**, working for a rich aristocrat, Lord Carnarvon. In 1914, Carter began looking for Tutankhamen's tomb. In 1922, clearing away rubble left by the tomb builders of a later king called Rameses VI, he found steps. These led down to a door. It was the entrance to a tomb, still closed up. It had not been opened for 3000 years.

Inside the tomb

When Carter opened the tomb, he saw 'wonderful things'. The tomb itself was fairly small. Within a golden **shrine**, in a **sarcophagus**, were three **coffins**. Finally, beneath the wrappings and the gold funeral mask, the **mummy** was revealed.

▶ Many of the precious items found in the tomb had been piled up hastily when it was closed up again after the robberies. Fortunately, the robbers had not returned.

Tutankhamen was not a great king. Yet his tomb treasures are the richest so far recovered from an Egyptian royal tomb. By studying them, historians have learned much more about life in Ancient Egypt. Finding Tutankhamen's tomb was a thrilling story of historical detective work, turning the forgotten boy-king into the most famous pharaoh of them all.

▶ Howard Carter opened the burial chamber on 17 February 1923. Hundreds of excited people waited to hear what he had found. He chipped a small hole and shone a torch inside to see 'an astonishing sight... a solid wall of gold'. It was Tutankhamen's gold-coated shrine.

Tutankhamen's treasures

Tutankhamen's treasures are displayed in the Egyptian Museum in Cairo, the capital of Egypt. Many of the objects are very delicate. Wood brought out of the tomb into the dry dessert air began to crack and shrink. Cloth and leather had rotted away. So had the threads of necklaces. Howard Carter made careful drawings of many objects, while Harry Burton took photographs. They put a number on each item to record exactly where it was found.

Glossary

Amen also spelt Amun and Amon, one of the most important gods in Egypt

archaeologist person who finds out about the past by looking for the remains of buildings and other objects, often beneath the ground

Aten Egyptian sun-god

bronze metal made by mixing melted copper and tin. It was used in ancient times for tools and weapons.

canopic decorated wooden, stone or clay jars or boxes, in which Egyptians put the four 'vital organs' of a dead person

chariot light cart with two wheels, pulled by horses

coffin box in which the body of a dead person is put

commoner person who is not an aristocrat or noble

counsellor a person who gives advice

embalmer person who preserves a dead body, as a mummy

excavating digging into the ground by archaeologists to uncover the ruins of a building or a tomb

genetic disease an illness which is passed on from parents to children.

hieroglyphs Egyptian picture-writing. The name means 'sacred writing' in Greek.

high priest the senior or most important priest

Hittites ancient, warlike people who lived in what is now Turkey. They invented iron tools.

ivory animal tooth. Ivory from elephant's tusks was carved to make ornaments and other things.

kilt skirt-like garment

lichen small, dry plant growing on rocks and trees, as soft as moss

linen cloth made from the woven fibres of the flax plant

monument building or statue built to remind people of a famous person or a famous event

mummy body of a dead person specially treated to stop it decaying

Nubians people from an area to the south of Egypt, in what is now Sudan. It was part of the Egyptian empire.

papyrus reed used to make paper

papyrus scrolls Egyptian books. Long strips of paper made from papyrus reed were wrapped up in a roll around a stick.

pharaoh king of Egypt

reed tall plant growing beside rivers and lakes

reign time during which a king or queen rules

sarcophagus stone coffin, often with other coffins inside it

scribe person trained to write. They often wrote government records and letters for other people.

shaduf simple machine for lifting water – a see-saw pole with a weight at one end and a bucket at the other

shrine specially holy place – a container with doors, inside which a god's statue or a royal coffin was kept

tablet small, flat piece of clay or stone used for writing on

temple building in which people worship a god or gods

tomb hole in the ground or in a rock cliff, or a special building, in which dead people are buried

treasurer government official in charge of money – spending it and collecting money in taxes

tribute gifts handed over by people to their rulers

Timeline

BC 3100	King Menes, the first pharaoh, rules all Egypt
2686–2181	Old Kingdom. Imhotep builds the first pyramid at Saqqara. King Khufu builds the Great Pyramid at Giza.
2040–1786	Middle Kingdom. First schools in Egypt. Amen of Thebes becomes an important god. City of Thebes becomes the capital.
1539–1075	New Kingdom
1390–1353	Reign of Amenhotep III
1352–1336	Reign of Akhenaten
1335–1333	Reign of Smenkhkare
1333–1323	Tutankhamen rules Egypt
1070–332	Libyan and Nubian kings rule Egypt. Assyrians invade Egypt. Persians also invade.
332	Alexander the Great conquers Egypt. He makes Alexandria the capital. Greek kings known as Ptolemies rule Egypt.
69–30	Life of Cleopatra, Queen of Egypt from 51 BC. After her death, Egypt is ruled by Rome.

Further reading & websites

Heinemann Explore History: Ancient Egypt, Jane Shuter, Heinemann Library, 2001

How Would You Survive as an Ancient Egyptian, Jacqueline Morley, Franklin Watts, 1993

Legacies from Ancient Egypt, Anita Ganeri, Belitha, 1999

Pharaohs and Embalmers, Anita Ganeri, Heinemann 1997

Tutankhamen, the Life and Death of a Boy king, Christine El Mahdy, Headline, 2000

Heinemann Explore – an online resource from Heinemann. For Key Stage 2 history go to *www.heinemannexplore.com*

www.ancientegypt.co.uk (British Museum)

www.discoveringegypt.com

Places to visit

British Museum, London

Tutankhamen Exhibition, Dorchester Museum, Dorset

Index

Titles in the Life and World of series include:

Hardback   0 431 14765 5

Hardback   0 431 14771 X

Hardback   0 431 14774 4

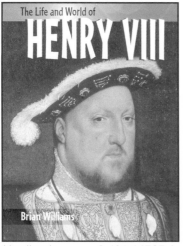

Hardback   0 431 14767 1

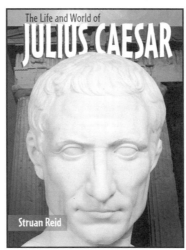

Hardback   0 431 14775 2

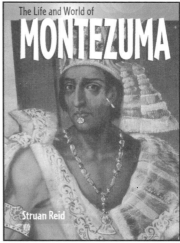

Hardback   0 431 14763 9

Hardback   0 431 14769 8

Hardback   0 431 14761 2

Find out about the other titles in this series on our website www.heinemann.co.uk/library